blooming

&

blossoming

Blooming & Blossoming

Copyright © 2023 Yamor Ada
Cover Design: Noemi De Feo

All rights reserved. No part of this book may be
reproduced or used in any manner without
the prior written permission of the copyright owner,
except for the use of brief quotations in a book review.

This book depicts events in the life of the author
according to their personal experiences and recollections.
All views are their own.

All rights reserved.
First paperback edition: June 2023
ISBN: 9798366023269

blooming & blossoming

a voyage of spiritual awakening

by: yamor

this book is dedicated to:

my mum; my boulder

a love that was lost at sea

the kindred spirits i've encountered along my journey

the island paradise that changed my life

thank you all for walking this path with me

i am forever grateful to have met you.

"whither the fates carry us."

the veil is lifted.

i see clearly.

i feel whole.

i feel home.

to whoever is reading this;

you are loved.

you are love.

i hope you can embark on this journey with me.

i hope my words can guide you home.

the journey

dawning   10

breaking   46

fading   84

awakening   104

returning   144

dawning

mirror soul.

the first ever time we locked eyes
i knew you were from a previous life
our cord pulled us in
and aligned our physical path

you felt like my home
my sanctuary

it's because you are me.

blaze.

i knew i had to explore your depths further when i saw you

your soul had the answers for mine

you were the earth in which my spirit wanted to explore

you were the solid ground for my campfire to burn

you were the foundation for my heart to set ablaze

you.

when i am with you
there is no need to be
anyone
anything
or anywhere else

no halving
just wholeness

two pieces of the puzzle coming together

thank you.

thank you for being a listening ear
without judgement, just presence
to be seen and heard for the first time
is all my inner child needed
you helped her hatch from her fragile shell
she always knew she had love within
but now was the time to extend that love in gratitude

you came at a time i least expected
among the chaos of my decluttering
my soul was making room for you
you connected me back to who i always was
the beautiful innocence of childhood
memories that were so deeply rooted
you showed me how to water them
and how to nourish its soil
because that love was never gone
it always remained at my core
you helped me to dig them out
and relive the days of the sweet little girl i once knew

kintsugi.

you don't pick and choose parts of me
like a broken machine

"which pieces do i throw,
which ones do i keep?"

you take me as i am
an imperfectly perfect whole being.

higher plane.

we spoke of our dreams
all our fantasies
what you'd do to me
on a parisian balcony.

stop over - meet me halfway
how much longer will i have to wait?

we promised we wouldn't let it sour
that we'd keep us alive
but we were strangers from the start
we didn't want to let our imaginations die

you stood next to me
picked me from a wild crowd
eyes blurred
words slurred
yet somehow
my path to you
was paved so clearly

the city of angels.

dazed

confused

but somehow found my way to you

let's make the most of this moment

if i had known it would've been the only time

maybe the only time in this lifetime

i would have held on

and cherished every part of your being.

it should have been you with me

on the lifeguard tower

watching the glistening moon on the waves crashing in

the luminescence of the pier lights

arms reaching out

the crisp air i'm inhaling in

smiling

yet longing

i thought i understood it,

maybe it was all too dream-like.

lust turning into resentment

hollowed out promises.

my wings are widespread

i'm ready to let go

there's nothing left

but acceptance.

destruction.

everything used to be so mundane
an infinite loop of numbness
over and over again

you were exactly the chaos and destruction i needed.

union.

i look in the mirror and see your reflection
i feel your presence filling up the room
like smoke flowing through my veins
and clouding my vision

i feel your touch as though you're here
the voices in your head are in mine
1 soul in 2 bodies
our flames intertwine

flames.

i go inward

where your lips are on mine

and we intertwine

your piercing eyes

feel like a soft touch

an emulation of the divine

inamorato.

i experienced the entire spectrum;

pleasure and pain.

you shined light to the darkness
all i tried to deny
you put me in line
and made me feel alive for the first time.

one way road.

we're of two different worlds
but of the same source
dispersing from physicality
we magnetised each other
and conjoined as one

welcome to the journey
it only goes one way

aren't you glad to be on it with me?

cosmic dust.

starting from zero

the rocket rises up to a place unknown

do you want to float around the stars with me?

a never-ending loop of this trajectory

if the powers that be

allow us to remain here

then i would take that chance

indefinitely.

but you always saw it as nonsensical.

eyes dazzled

losing control

i need something to hold onto

dearly

desperately

before we disperse into a million pieces.

my insides are set ablaze

a moment of pure elation

suddenly, it all turns into cosmic dust

but somehow i'm ready to rise up

and start the loop

all

over

again

island.

i landed in paradise
and instantly felt home
you felt familiar
comforting.
like when i was a child
in my family holiday home
those summers with my family
on the clearest beaches in turkey
it was all a reminder
of what i always was.

the first night felt peaceful
the faint sound of crickets in the distance
gazing at the clearest starry sky
on the balcony at night

it was a home that wasn't my own
but felt so close to my soul.

i then realised
that no matter where i was on this earth
the feeling of home
was something i was carrying in me all along.

emmeline lestrange.

sandy skin

gritty hair

no tomorrow

no yesterday

simply today

the ocean is the only thing

that can wash all my worries away

nectarines.

the sandy footpaths

swinging on the hammock

pushing each other in the pool

the smell of grandma's food

evenings at the beach

the family around the table

tan skin and freckles

figs and nectarines

the sunny balcony

vines hanging from the veranda

sea salty hair

the sound of crickets

afternoon naps

feeding the animals

watering the garden

child-like.

we shared with each other
like little children
getting excited over ice cream
although we were from different worlds
we were the same at heart

we had no one else to share this with
so we found it in each other instead
an innocence that is a child's core
but blackens as they mature

you were pure love to me.

the unexplainable.

there's so much to be said, yet the words just don't want to flow out.
sometimes i smile and drop into the feeling of it instead,
and i know that it is enough.

that the words are not needed, nor does it need to be understood or analysed. the vastness of the feeling running through my body is like an electrical current, filling up every cell with divine light.

there is no explanation for it, there's only feeling it.

it's a feeling of freedom, of eternity, my childhood memories;
a sweet nectar of presence.
like biting into a warm nectarine as the juices flow down your chin
and onto your chest.
like the salt on your skin after swimming in the sea
as you bask in the warmth of the midday sun.
like the sound of laughter in the distance
or the sounds of children play fighting.

all the moments in life that cannot be forgotten,
because they are eternal.

the only things temporary are these words
that are trying to explain the unexplainable.

aeon.

the infinite horizon was behind you
my focus then shifted to your eyes

i saw the divine for the first time.

ascension.

i feel closer and closer to god
each time i see you

how could i ever feel alone
when i know you're always with me in my heart?

your essence is everything, everywhere

a sweet melodic hum of birds
the trees swaying in the breeze
your soft ocean eyes
and that gentle smile

you are divinity here on earth.

the only exception.

we are just guests on this earth
no one is ours forever
nothing is ours to keep

but for you
my guilty pleasure
i'd bend the laws of nature

cliff.

i stand on the edge looking down

freedom i have never felt
air i have never breathed
the deepest hue of blue
i have ever seen
nothingness; just my being

undisturbed peace.

but you pull me from the edge
the shadows of fear paint the sky black
if only you pulled me in the same way
into your arms instead

alive.

if someone asked me;
"if you could only choose one moment from the past
that you could relive, what would it be?"

it would be the time dusk was approaching
i was walking towards the edge of the cliff
the hues of blue felt like heaven
the ocean waves were crashing in
and it was the first time i ever held my heart
felt pure bliss
breathed in
and smiled.

it was the first time i felt alive.

your hurt is mine.

when you pulled me from the edge of the cliff
i could feel your anxiety
the moments of frustration
and snapping
weren't directed at me
but it was a deep hurt
that wanted release
the pain you felt at that time
although it wasn't mine
i felt it like it was
because i saw myself in you.

so we're no different you see
we're just made of up the same energy.

midnight.

it's midnight on the balcony
the moonlight engulfs us
the soft breeze
whistles in the trees

smoke in the air
inhaling to numb
exhaling to empty

it's just us

looking into nothingness

the silence swallows us whole.

mourning doves.

a night so cold and bleak

with its empty streets

you were minutes away

but the sweet voice of jhenè

and the trees leaves whistling to me

were my only real company

my shadow.

your love was harsh
but it softened me

experience.

there always was a ticking time bomb between us.
we knew we'd have to part ways, and we did multiple times
but i am so thankful you took me to your home with you,
before the final departure.
through witnessing your life, your family, your land, i slowly started to connect the pieces to find my own. it felt like a dream.
you were taking me through my childhood memories.
i didn't quite grasp it at the time, but i now know it in all its glory.
that i was longing for love and home for so long,
but it was with me all along.
that the love of these memories and the people that have touched us are always etched in our hearts, even if they depart.
seeing your grandparents, swimming in the sea, watching tv in the lounge with the midday sun glowing through the window, the endless car journeys, sitting on the edges of cliffs, small towns and neighbourhoods, and so much nature all around.
every single moment painted me the picture of my own essence;
the essence that can never die and is eternal. it is love.
you helped me find home. i hope that maybe i helped you find yours - or that you will someday.

i will never forget what you did for me. maybe this life or the next.

until we meet again.

ammonite.

once upon a time
we walked on these rocks together

unearthing pandora's box
i excavated what was preserved
to relive those days

the traces of you are imprinted
like beautiful etchings on my bones
crumbling's compressed
in fossilised formations

what is left of you
are artefactual remains
at the museum of innocence

atlantic.

to the bluest of blues:

i dropped my heart in your waters
and you cleansed my vessel
pumped new blood in my veins
ignited my insides
filled my body with your light

thank you for
healing me
purifying me
awakening me

water.

the water moves in many motions
it comes in and parts ways
despite wherever it flows
there's serenity in knowing
it'll always connect our souls

goodbye nirvana.

the thunderstorm gave me strength
the rain cried for my departure
the rainbow spread out its hope
the sunset kissed me goodbye

empty seats across the plane
dark like a black womb
i placed my headphones on
curled up in a tiny ball
and awaited to be reborn.

flux.

death is bliss

a peaceful departure back home

but what's painful is not knowing

if your leaving

was a mere farewell

or the final goodbye.

breaking

mirror reflections.

when i looked in the mirror
i saw your face
and endless tears fell from my eyes

i only ever saw you.

miles apart yet it felt like you were in that room with me.

did you not see me in your own reflection
or was it always just about you?

woe is you, after all.

did you once break through to your heart centre
and clip away the hard-shelled armour?

did you ever soften at the sight of your own humanness?

it doesn't hurt to break a smile.

pity party.

i wonder if you were too busy in your own world to even see

did you notice how i tended to and kissed your injuries?

how i hugged you through the dark and rainy nights with
all your tears running down your cheeks?

you ran away when you saw my wounds.

but i guess nurturing yours was like tending to my own

you are me, after all.

the light i provided shone onto the darkness
that you were absorbed in
you knew you had nowhere to run
you can't outrun yourself

stop the pity party and look inward

surrender.

it's time to face the love you had always feared.

a piece of me.

how can i avoid you when you are everywhere?
the air i breathe, the sun's rays and moons beams.
i can't escape you, because it would be like escaping me.

did you lose your mind the way i did for you?
love supposedly makes people go crazy.

did you cry for me?
did you die for me?
i die a little more each day.

i really hate you. i hope you know that.

i bet you're only thinking of your own miseries right now whilst i wallow in both of ours.

until next time.

love is so bittersweet, isn't it?

for how would we know love if we didn't know loss?

how could i have understood love if i did not grieve it?

i knew what it meant to love after losing many people
but your hit was the most crippling.

us humans are funny beings
we're never truly present with people in their totality
yet away from them
we miss them dearly
even the messiest parts

we are creatures of many polarities
yet they go hand in hand
because their beauty is in their harmony.

fortress.

do you marvel at the world as deeply as i do?

you always were a broody moongazer
and i never really got a glimpse into your inner world
yet i could always feel it in my own space
i guess the words were not needed

the distance spoke louder than anything else could.

the empty spaciousness between us was deafening.

like a fortress you had placed to keep me away from your heart
that i was trying to connect to

but i know i touched that heart space.

i felt it expand.

even if you tried to close it back up
and protect it with all your might
once there is even the slightest entrance of light
you cannot go back.

bittersweet.

you took a piece of me for yourself
but gave me back a piece of you
do i thank you
or live on hating you?

effy stonem.

i painted a picture of you
with all that i wanted us to be

and after a while i replaced the memories
convincing myself that it's what we really were

the pain started to fade.

liberation.

i'm glad you were the one that let me go
because i never would have had the guts to do it myself

thank you for freeing us.

untethering.

the day you broke my heart
was the day i broke open

i galloped freely into the horizon

looking glass.

there's nowhere to take cover

in the house of mirrors

try to run

but you'll end up running into yourself

you can shatter the glass

and fracture every part of your being

but the shards are still there

waiting for you

to pick them up from the floor

and slowly reassemble the pieces

plucking up the courage this time

to look into your eyes

what do you see?

is your own reflection startling?

lighthouse.

the lights warn me
flashing before my eyes
rushing to my aid
but i ignore the signs

the waves are overwhelming
the storms try to capsize me
but i keep sailing
navigating through the intensity

uncertainty

will i make it out the other side?

again the signals warn me
it's not too late to turn back
i ignore my compass

and eventually crash.

covet.

you joined my timeline

from a different realm

tainted my shine

sucked the light from my essence

headed back to your world

like it was all fine

impermanence.

you came and you left
it's like you were never here to begin with

it was always just me.

shamaness.

i saw your wounds
that i so badly wanted to mend
a golden heart on a silver platter
right in front of you
but you didn't see
you weren't ready to receive

mesopotamia.

when i looked into your eyes
i ceased to be
you looked into mine
but didn't see

why don't you stop running?
why are you so scared of magic?

give in and drink the elixir of life
it's better on the other side
if not through this avatar
then there's always next time.

sea salt.

all i wanted was your nectar

but you stung me

like salt on a wound

and parched

every

layer

of

life

all i wanted was your sweetness

but you blinded me

like acid

scarring

all

my

tissue

i longed for your sugar coating

and to nestle me in your hive

you dried up every part of me

left

senseless

inside

empty promises.

he promised her the world
but threw it right back in her face

she mended her own broken heart
with the promises she made for herself

outpour.

i nurtured you from an empty cup
as you poured yourself into me

my cup overflowed for you.

elysia.

an underworld of secrets

caves of serenity

prancing around arcadia

the land you had promised me

a girl can only dream.

goddess.

next time a man tells me
he will give me the world
my response will be:

i am the world.

scars.

maybe your former crocodile tears
are now ones of purifying waters

do they burn your skin when they release?

because the tears i have cried for you
have left scars on my cheeks.

purge.

the tears were acidic and warm

like they were waiting a lifetime to pour out

poison.

everything you touch seems to die
like the honey drip turning into poison
in-between my thighs

venom.

your charm was sweet

but your sting even sweeter

luring me into your trap

marking your territory with your fangs

sucking the soul out of my vessel

leaving me lusting for more

possession.

all i ever wanted was your sweet embrace
was it too much to ask for?

a gentle kiss
or even just a thought of me
all you did was extract my spirit
to fuel your own lifeless body

ouroboros.

you were the master of telling fables
like the one about the woman you loved
the same you carelessly let go of
a serpent that eats its own tail
writing the opening act and end scene
are you amused by your own play?
your cycle of self-absorption caught up to you
all to your hearts content.

tourniquet.

with your wraith wrapped around you
you were haunted by deceit
blinded by your woeful perception
biting the only hand within reach
the one that bandaged your lesions

your insides vacant from the beginning
there was no need to stop the bleeding

a body that was always extinct.

kiss of judas.

my birthmark
is a reminder
from where you stabbed me
in a past life
over and over and over

your forked tongue
punctured my lungs
pierced through my spleen
life pouring out
bleeding me dry

there's always next time
to be my remedy.

battleground.

you used your sword to fend off
those that fought by your side
your shielded armour
failed to protect you
the shock waves were stronger
and they penetrated through
cracking you from the inside
breaking the one place you were trying to shelter
stop holding onto the fractured remnants
the battle is over

admit defeat.

samskara.

remember my embrace

when all the other arms pushed you away

memento mori.

as a piece of me dies each day
you've been dying along with it

garden of eden.

how does it feel to be in paradise
when i am stuck in this zombieland?
how does it feel to be surrounded by crystal clear waters
the glittering suns heat on your back
and the palm trees all lined up in unison perfectly?
how does it feel to be in the land of the gods and holy spirits,
whilst i am here inhaling dust and smoke
on the wasteland of walking corpses?
how does it feel to fall asleep to the lull of tree frogs
and wake up to the melody of singing birds?
heaven must be treating you real good.

but i know you're miserable deep down.
you have the garden of eden at your feet
yet you are crippled by the blackness
of your own mind to see its enchantment.
i see the beauty in the dirt of these city streets
and millions of lost souls
that walk in doom and gloom by me each day.
you see, that is the difference between you and me
i have managed to find peace amongst chaos

have you found peace in the place
that is nothing short of abundant of it?

frequencies.

we are not the same, you and me.
do you feel whole and complete in your state of pity?
you can call me all high and mighty
and you bet i am on this higher vibrational frequency

if you want to access this energy,
how about switching the dial on yours?
tune into a new radio station
perhaps to the one where you experience some time alone

does your own company fulfil you now?
it's just what you always wanted.
is it unnerving? unsettling? good.
at least you feel something for the first time.

maybe there were nights when you hated it so much
so you changed the dial in panic.
i felt you change the channel. it hit me like a wave.
i can feel when we're on the same channel.
i get surprised when you tune yours up higher to match mine.
but you'll get bored again. i know you too well.

just know that i'll always be on the same channel,
if you ever change your mind.

phantoms of the past.

does my ghost still haunt your land?

does all the small-town talk make you feel alone?

when you drive to work every day, do you see the timeline shift
to the summer when we were wild and free?

do you sit under the trees and talk to the leaves
as though they were me?

do your insides feel numb when you stand at the edge of the cliff
and look out to the sea?

do you feel me visit you in your lonely moments?

or are you still enjoying the company of your own demons?

tell me.

you must feel like a king in your tower,
overlooking the gardens of paradise.
how does it feel to drive by the hibiscus lined bushes
and the smell of the sea salt every day?
it must be gentle to you.
are you happy in your white collar and suit?
has the money made you feel secure?
how about your heart?
is it being nurtured by another woman?
did she strip away your false self?
or did she comply like a good girl that does everything you ask?
you are the king, after all.
how are your fancy dinners and the clinks of champagne glasses?
have you finally satisfied your greed of material desire?
are you still hungry for more?
do your friends who 'talk about nothing' still do just that?
are they helping you to grow or sink further
into the world of their despair?
how is the island life treating you?
are you enjoying the boat parties
and drowning yourself in sweet spirits?
despite being in the abundance of water, are you still thirsty?

tell me, have you figured out what's missing?

fading

eternity.

baby,
please remember who you are
remember your true self.

i want you to know
that i will love you for eternity.

even if you don't remember in this lifetime
i will always wait for you
you remembered in a previous one
you'll remember again

as long as it takes
i'm always here.

remember;
"you've got me."

linger.

how do i stop myself
from your linger?
you are everywhere i go
everywhere i look
i lay on the grass
and you're there next to me
holding my hand

how do i stop the incessant chatter inside
whilst still keeping a piece of you?
maybe i enjoy your presence
it's comforting
maybe that's why i still hold you close
it's all i have left of you

linger a little longer, my love.

creation.

i remember one night
when we were on a cliff
gazing at the starlights
and i closed my eyes
inhaled deeply
and the horizon had shot an arrow
of white light through my chest

these are the moments
that will be etched in my mind
and my heart
and will remain with me
for the rest of my life

and as the years continue on by
through it all
i'm grateful it was you that was by my side

utopia.

i would be transported to other worlds in my sleep
one where we were wearing white linen
twinkling eyes and endless smiles
our angel wings carried us gracefully over the ocean
holding hands and looking out to the horizon

please don't wake me up from this dream.

buried alive.

buried relics
waiting to be resurfaced
hoping to see the light

the mourning silence
stories left unvoiced
the words that were unspoken
awaiting the breaking of dawn
needing to flow through
like water through a flume

open the channel
help me resurrect
what was never dead

phoenix.

there is no need
to wait for death
because with each passing day
being torn apart from you
was tormenting
judgement day came to me
and what i had seen
were the heavens reuniting
what was meant to be
the real death
is love's departure
the playground
of fire and ice
is right beneath our feet

mirage.

do you remember me?
do you remember my intricacies?

i remember running my fingertips along your chest
marking my territory gently

your broad shoulders
like protective angel wings wrapped around me
firm, yet nurturing

i always felt held in your embrace.

like a dream.

there are parts of you that are so vivid
and parts so faint
it all feels as though it was just yesterday.

nostalgia.

the memories in my mind roll like a film strip
i've learned that it's not you i miss
but the feelings the nostalgia brings

timelines.

a memory that catches you by surprise

and makes you pause and reflect

the spark of reliving it again

is better than what any photo could ever encapsulate

tune into your heart

and feel it's tender embrace

the disconnect.

how strange it can be
to go from the sweetest melody
to disharmony

the dismantling
of what was once whole

all i can discern
are the faint memories

unrequited.

it's hard to comprehend
how we can love someone
in their totality
that your heart had the capacity
to break open
and pour out so effortlessly
there are no barriers
or limits
when two hearts
amalgamate as one
and pump in unison
to the sound of
soft thumping
and gentle pulsations
like your first home
until one decides
to rattle the harmony
pulling apart
the heart strings
an arrhythmic beat
a breakout of war
fragments of flesh
and a pool of blood
where it was once composure

evanesce.

people come

only to go

like stars

that dissipate

just like us

we came to compress

only to disperse again

sempiternal.

my eyes flicker

an iridescence that gleams over them

like the click of a viewmaster

moments of nostalgia

but all that's here is now.

echo.

you were an echo of all my shadows

cracking open the seed from the darkest pit

for my roots to spiral upwards and flourish

my anima.

there was a time
when i remembered all the details of you

you're nothing but my shadow now.

a memory.

i listen to the breeze hit the golden leaves
and watch the soft sway of the branches

there is nothing left of you
but god itself

iron sharpens iron.

i hope that one day you're illuminated
the way your love has illuminated me

i hope you are guided to what you already know.

awakening

the calling.

the howl you can no longer ignore

is rooted deep inside of you

it echoes throughout your body

so are the answers you're searching for

unravel.

i'm tired of walking
but my legs aren't tired of me
the road seems to be a never-ending stretch
but if i have no fight left
i'm as good as dead
i don't know where i am now
but i'd rather aimlessly wander
with hope
with the possibility
of what awaits at the end for me

martyr.

sometimes my feet have a mind of their own
numb from all the pitfalls
they work quickly to save others
from stumbling over their own two feet
but theirs are already firmly planted
somehow i still run to their aid

the bottom of this dark well
has left me paralysed
surely they've noticed their stagnancy

will anyone come to rescue me?

rubble.

continually escaping
the trails of wreckage i'd leave behind
you confronted me
and made me face the debris

i didn't expect you to appear
nor to throw me a rope
and pull me up
from the ditch i had been stuck in

it turns out it's much sweeter
to be where you were standing

shedding.

you chipped away
at my blackened armour
with your chisel
revealing what was always inside
but locked away so tight

grief.

i'm grieving the old me.

grieving the clinging of my old identity.
grieving the person i thought i was
grieving the person i thought i should be
grieving the disintegrating of all the structures
that no longer support me

grieving what once was
but is no longer meant to be
grieving the destruction and chaos
that has crumbled me
grieving all that has brought me down to my knees

i surrender to the new me.

release.

the pain of awakening

is not a blanket of sorrow

nor a ditch of despair

but one that's unbinding

from all that was inscribed

awaiting you is the other side

no turning back.

the old self wails and pleads for safety
she says she wants to protect me
but to go back to her destruction
would be a disservice to the innocent girl
that i kept locked inside for so long

the more i step forward
the more i step back into the real me

the one i'm now setting free.

silence speaks.

i pray and give love
to my being
for the pain to release
because in the
stillness
surrender
and silence
comes the peace.

kensho.

witness

the old self wither

it'll beg for mercy

don't give into its weep

let it disintegrate

and evaporate

because it's no longer serving

your supreme being

any stagnancy

is a lack of light entering

so simply let go

and move in forward momentum

to your sovereignty

chimera.

playing

dress up

show up

done up

made up

have you ever stopped to think;

this is what disrupts

the light from inside

tune into the unsettling quivers from your gut

because it never lies

you'll dream of having this or that

where does it end?

we can't have it all

the world isn't that kind

it'll always feel so afar

do you want to truly feel alive?

then wipe the slate clean

set the old ways on fire

and let the structures perish

longing.

yearning to recreate that safe space i once felt
a deep longing for a place that shelters me
trying to escape where i am in this moment
grasping to anything outside of me

frantically.
fearfully.

i've been trying to run away from
the very thing that i'm chasing after

i am my home.

paradox.

when i let you go
there was an emptiness where i felt freedom
a numbness where i also felt alive

you are nothing but a memory now
it's all faded into blackness
sometimes you like to make a guest appearance
from my shadows
as a reminder to never forget
my deepest fear
of forgetting
it's a daily conquering

there is a sacrifice to be paid in everything
losing you meant finding love
in its purest form

all that was agonising
was the reviving of me

here.

nowhere to be but here
no one to be but me

untamed.

no one can put out my flames
nor make me feel small
i reclaim my intuition
and listen to my hearts wild call

i howl with the wolves
bask in the sunshine
connect to my source
receive from my divine

i sing with the birds
dance beneath the trees
ground myself to earth

i'm finally free

mother gaia.

here's me worrying about my puny little heart
broken by insignificant men
whilst she's been bent and broken
time and time again

crumbled into dust
yet somehow moulded herself back like clay

she is my boulder
firmly planted
i've never known anyone stronger on this earth

sorceress.

she lives in the otherworld

she flows with the mystery of it all

she is unafraid to stand in her own power

she is rooted to the earth

she is in her own knowing

she transforms herself and those around her

she has an intuition sharper than a blade

she is the holder of secrets

she is independent in nature

she is interconnected with other beings

she is selfless

she is giving

she is passion

she is wisdom

she is healing

comfort zone.

i stopped looking outside for a comfort zone
when i realised that i was already whole
i quietened my mind and looked inwards
and found a comforting place called home

the city.

a city full of people
yet so isolated from one and other
hibernating in the winter
shielded from each other

when the rebirth begins
and the spring flowers bloom
the sun brings us together
and we hatch out of our cocoons

return home.

i funnel through the background noise
returning to my calm
i'm safe here.

i am not in this alone
and neither are you.
we are all misguided
wandering aimlessly

or perhaps just misdirected;
because we all have a home to go back to.

when we are surrounded in clatter
sometimes home is in the midst of the chaos

find the still
in all that surrounds you.

witness.

that is the journey of this life;

to always return home

no matter what the situation outside of us is

non duality.

once you're awake

you can see both the dark and the light so clearly

they're woven together so intricately

one will always call out for the other

and every time one gets a little lost

it'll find its way right back into the others' arms

the in-between.

the mind is clouded by linearity
trying to get from point a to b
yearning to escape the place it's in currently

go within
you'll see it's all intertwined

embrace the journey

the unknown.

my heart longs for the past
and hopes for the future

journeying.

your life turns upside down
and will never go back to how it was
yet it becomes
what it was always meant to

forgiveness.

for the times you held your breath in silence
for the times you pushed your feelings down
for the times you should have left but didn't
for the times you did not understand your value

for how could you have possibly known the journey
you were about to embark?

you are a brave soul navigating ferocious waters.

the truth.

unravel the layers of skin
that weigh you down into a pit
you'll hear the howl
and the answers deep within

stillness.

in the stillness of now
the earth speaks to me
getting lost in the trails
watching butterflies land on trees

there's no greater abundance
than the absence of thinking
surrender to what is
and feel the bliss deepening within

severing.

how easily beauty can be missed

when your mind is constantly in the abyss

witness what's in front of you

by severing the ties

that anchor you down

swim up to the surface

and surrender to solace

chrysalis.

the pain of awakening
letting go of everything you knew
every narrative you ever wrote
every play you acted out
is the hardest you will endure
because it is pain that is actually felt
deeply at your core.

it's not a void
or a numbness
but a discomforting blossoming
an expansive opening.

crack open your shell
expand your chest
and let your wings soar

transcending.

hold your heart
and feel endlessly

open your eyes
and see clearly

quieten your mind
and hear the truth undeniably

arise.

ascending
into a higher state of being
letting go of all you knew
feels gut wrenching

cutting
the cords of resistance
unlearning everything is scary
but equally liberating

accepting
the new path you're taking
it's a part of the greater plan
your light is calling
arise.

crystalline.

i quieten my mind
and get hypnotised
the deepest sensations
an opening of a portal
transcending time
tuning into my senses
into the everlasting now.

electromagnetic.

white waves in the cosmos
boundlessly scattered stardust
your magnetic pull allured me
wrapping your cord around my neck
marking your territory

i can feel your field opening

will you let love in?

siren.

are you afraid of me, darling?
follow my sweet lullaby
to the abyssal depths of the sea
if you want to be enchanted
then escape with me
listen to your calling
of your inner alchemy
keep swimming
until you submerge
to the bed of dark blue hues
a triangle of lapis lazuli
it's a world far from the one you knew

are you ready for your destiny?

lotus.

rise out of the chaos

rise into love

become love.

threshold.

they say ignorance is bliss

but release your pride

let it crash and burn

yield to your call

because crossing the threshold

will be your sweetest fall

returning

thorns.

the splinters in my heart were removed

and i was washed with your blood

it was catalyst of a deeper love

a grief that blossomed infinity

a forever lasting unhindered peace.

for love.

you hold a heart so big in a chest
that was blackened by shadows
you managed to love someone
so deeply and unconditionally
despite your own heart being caged
be proud of yourself
for opening your heart for the first time
and maybe the love wasn't reciprocated
in the way you anticipated
but never give up on yourself
please don't in the name of love
the source of all.

you did the bravest thing a person could do
you tore your heart
out of its fragile shell
all to mend the other
it's time for you
to place that heart back in your own chest
and let it love you back

love.

i will never apologise

for leading my life with a heart wide open

and love that runs so deep

gratitude.

i have found a love for life
one that needs no understanding
but just to simply smile about it all

shaping.

give thanks to all that has

hurt you

bent you

broken you

shattered you

dissolved you

diminished you

belittled you

ridiculed you

abandoned you

shaped you.

sunshine.

the grey clouds
that followed me all my life
have finally drifted away
now all i see above me
are sun rays

a new chapter.

she breathed deeply and smiled
because she knew that she had just read the final word

the last chapter.

she didn't want to read the same book again and again
there are endless ways she could interpret it
but she already knows how this story goes.

she wanted a new story
one that isn't written by someone else
she told herself that this time
she's going to write it herself

destino.

a dream is a seed planted in your spirit

align.

the flashes of my future self are so vivid, so close

i feel the touch of her skin as my own

remembering.

for so long i thought i was trying to escape reality
but now that i have finally found home
i know that it was a journey of remembering me

navigation.

how can you possibly be lost in life,
when your heart is the roadmap?

anchor.

a guidance of the heart

a warm smile

not speaking

not controlling

it's understanding

and accepting

the self as you are

the other as they are

surrender and faith

complete grace

infinite and everlasting

not doing or needing

it breaks you open

and fills you with light

it's a warming sunset

and dark tint of the night

love is just being.

the now.

the past is there for a lesson
the future is there for purpose
the present is your guiding anchor

confluence.

there are many paths
to the stationary point of love
like two rivers flowing
ultimately converging as one body of water

we can move independently in vain
like parallel lines that don't cross over
but the ultimate equilibrium is inevitable

like the ease of stillness
in the midst of the storm
you will always spiral back
to your north star

memorial.

my story is pretty magical

but it's just another drop in the ocean

soon it will be washed away

like a message in a bottle

adrift at sea and forgotten

boundless.

explore the limitless versions of your essence
unearth the ever-expanding versions of your being
connect boundlessly to your core
you are eternity in human form.

prakriti.

our hearts will connect in unison

and when it does it'll be pure

not desperate

just know that my heart is open

and waiting to reconcile

to heal this wound

for our higher selves

and greater good

but most importantly

for this divine journey

of selflessness

and ascension

one.

one day
we'll look into each other's eyes
like it's the first time
and through the glass of mine
you won't just look
but you'll see
your own reflection

shed the withering petals

and bloom into your higher self

may we rise together.

about the author

yamor is a poet, writer, and creator.

blooming & blossoming is her first self-published collection
of poetry and prose; rawly and vulnerably navigating themes of
love, loss, healing, and awakening.

she is an advocate for feminine self-empowerment and loves exploring
the depths of her experiences as a woman. as a student of life, she is
passionate about continuously learning, spreading wisdom and the
message of hope and love on her spiritual journey.

from her heart to yours.

Printed in Great Britain
by Amazon